EYEWITNESS
Activity

WEATHER
WATCHER

by John Woodward

REVISED EDITION

Editor Virien Chopra
Assistant Art Editor Nidhi Rastogi
Senior Editors Carron Brown, Bharti Bedi
Senior Art Editors Sheila Collins, Nishesh Batnagar
DTP Designer Pawan Kumar
Senior DTP Designer Harish Aggarwal
Pre-production Manager Balwant Singh
Producer, Pre-production Gillian Reid
Senior Producer Rita Sinha
Managing Editors Linda Esposito, Kingshuk Ghoshal
Managing Art Editors Philip Letsu, Govind Mittal
Jackets Assistant Claire Gell
Jacket Designers Laura Brim, Dhirendra Singh
Managing Jackets Editor Saloni Singh
Jacket Design Development Manager Sophia MTT
Publisher Andrew Macintyre
Associate Publishing Director Liz Wheeler
Design Director Stuart Jackman
Publishing Director Jonathan Metcalf

ORIGINAL EDITION

Produced for Dorling Kindersley Ltd by
Cooling Brown Ltd:
Creative Director Arthur Brown
Editor Kesta Desmond

For Dorling Kindersley Ltd:
Senior Editor Shaila Brown
Senior Art Editor Stefan Podhorodecki
Managing Editor Linda Esposito
Managing Art Editor Diane Thistlethwaite
Publishing Managers Caroline Buckingham, Andrew Macintyre
Jacket Designer Neal Cobourne
Jacket Copywriter Adam Powley
Jacket Editor Mariza O'Keeffe
Publishing Director Laura Buller
Production Controller Erica Rosen
Picture Researcher Ceila Dearing
DK Picture Library Rose Horridge
DTP Designer Siu Chan
Photography Dave King
Consultant Lisa Burke

First published in Great Britain in 2006
This edition first published in Great Britain in 2015 by
Dorling Kindersley Limited, 80 Strand, London, WC2R ORL

Copyright © 2006, © 2015 Dorling Kindersley Limited
A Penguin Random House Company
2 4 6 8 10 9 7 5 3 1
001–274461–Sep/2015

A CIP catalogue record for this book is available from
the British Library.

ISBN 978-0-2411-8543-8

Colour reproduction by Alta Image Ltd, London, UK
Printed in China

A WORLD OF IDEAS:
SEE ALL THERE IS TO KNOW
www.dk.com

Contents

Weather and climate

We are all affected by the weather. At its worst, weather can destroy cities and cause devastating floods. At its best, it can turn a simple picnic into a magical experience. But weather is also fascinating in its own right. Why does the wind blow? How do clouds form? What causes lightning? How is a rainbow made? You can find out by trying a few experiments and building some simple weather-watching instruments. You may even learn how to predict what the weather may do next.

Heavenly beauty

The weather is more than just wind, rain, and snow. It also includes some stunning atmospheric effects that can transform the sky. These include rainbows, sunsets, and flashes of lightning. This glorious sunset was photographed near Tierra del Fuego at the southern tip of South America.

World climates

The average weather of any place is described as its climate. The weather in California, USA, for example, is usually warm and dry, so it has a warm, dry climate. By contrast, New Zealand has a cool, damp climate. A region's climate is affected by how far it is from the equator, among other things. Climates can be described in many ways, but the climates of the world are often divided into five types. These are tropical, dry, warm temperate, cool temperate, and Arctic. Each climate type has many variations.

Tropical climate ▲
Near the equator, the heat and moisture in the air causes the formation of huge clouds and heavy rain. This encourages the growth of lush rainforests. Shown above is a rainforest in Costa Rica.

Dry climate ▲
In many regions, but mainly near the tropics, very dry air prevents the formation of clouds and rain. This leads to the development of deserts, such as the cactus deserts of the southwest USA.

STORM RELIEF

We all know what we mean by good weather and bad weather. For most of us, good weather is warm and sunny, while bad weather is cold and wet. But some people's bad weather is other people's good weather. For example, people who go skiing look forward to winter, and some people even enjoy thunderstorms. Rainstorms can be destructive, but they bring new life to places that suffer drought. In parts of southern Asia, the arrival of heavy monsoon rain at the end of the dry season is a reason for celebration, even though it can cause serious floods.

Monsoon rain ▶
Indian children make the most of a flash flood at the start of the wet season.

Warm temperate climate ▲
Some regions, for example, southern Australia, enjoy a warm temperate climate, where the weather is usually warm and sunny but there is enough rain to grow crops.

Cool temperate climate ▲
Places such as New Zealand and northwest Europe have cool summers but quite mild winters. The weather tends to be very changeable. Plants grow well because there is plenty of rain.

Arctic climate ▲
In the polar regions the weather is always cold, and temperatures fall well below freezing in winter. This leads to the growth of thick ice sheets, fringed by treeless, grassy land known as tundra.

The Earth is surrounded by a mixture of gases that we call air, and these form the atmosphere. Most of the air is in the lower atmosphere – in a layer called the troposphere – and at higher altitudes there is not enough air to breathe. The air in the troposphere is warmed from below by heat rising off the sun-warmed oceans and continents. The heat sets the air in motion and carries water vapour up into the sky, and this causes the world's weather.

Layered atmosphere

The atmosphere consists of four main layers. The lowest is the troposphere and is only 16 km (10 miles) thick. Air movements in this layer cause the weather. Above this is the stratosphere, the mesosphere, and then the thermosphere, which fades into the vacuum of space.

THE OZONE LAYER

The Sun's rays include a lot of invisible infrared and ultraviolet radiation (light). The infrared keeps us warm, but the ultraviolet is dangerous. It gives us sunburn and deadly skin cancer. Luckily, most of the ultraviolet radiation is absorbed by a gas called ozone, which forms a thin layer in the atmosphere about 25 km (16 miles) above the ground. Without this protective layer, animals would not be able to live on land, and human life could not exist.

Ozone hole ▲
Every winter a "hole" appears in the ozone layer over Antarctica. The hole appears in blue in this satellite image. It is caused by the lack of sunlight in winter, but it may be made bigger by air pollution.

120 km
(75 miles)

110 km
(68 miles)

100 km
(62 miles)

90 km
(56 miles)

80 km
(50 miles)

70 km
(43 miles)

60 km
(37 miles)

50 km
(31 miles)

40 km
(25 miles)

30 km
(19 miles)

20 km
(12 miles)

10 km
(6 miles)

Sea
level

Jet airliners
fly in the
troposphere

**Height above
sea level**

THIN AIR

The higher you climb, the thinner the air becomes. This is because there is less weight of air to squeeze it together, (less air pressure). Just 10 km (6 miles) above sea level, the air is too thin to keep people alive. Some mountains are more than 8 km (5 miles) high, and near their peaks there is barely enough air to breathe.

Life support ▲
Most mountaineers use breathing apparatus when they climb the highest mountains, such as Mount Everest in the Himalayas.

Thermosphere
The outer layer of the atmosphere starts about 80 km (50 miles) up, and gets hotter with height.

Aurora occurs in the thermosphere

Most meteors burn up in the atmosphere

Mesosphere
The mesosphere starts about 48 km (30 miles) up, and gets cooler the higher you go.

Ozone layer in the stratosphere absorbs harmful solar radiation

Stratosphere
The stratosphere starts 10–20 km (6–12 miles) above sea level, and gets warmer near the top.

Troposphere
This is the layer in which we live. It gets cooler near the top.

60°C (140°F)
-10°C (14°F)
-80°C (-112°F)
-90°C (-130°F)
-80°C (-112°F)
-50°C (-58°F)
-30°C (-22°F)
-10°C (14°F)
-20°C (-4°F)
-40°C (-40°F)
-60°C (-76°F)
-60°C (-76°F)
15°C (59°F)

Average temperature

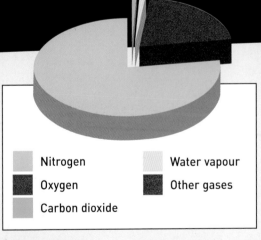

Nitrogen
Oxygen
Carbon dioxide
Water vapour
Other gases

Gas mixture

Air is made of a mixture of gases. Its two main ingredients are nitrogen (78 per cent) and oxygen (21 per cent). The other 1 per cent consists of carbon dioxide and other gases, such as argon, neon, helium, and ozone. There is also a small, but variable amount of water vapour mixed with the air.

Moving air

Near the equator, the heat of the Sun makes warm air rise and flow towards the cold polar regions. The rising air is replaced by cooler air flowing from the poles towards the equator. This global air flow cools down the hottest parts of the Earth, and warms up the coldest parts. But the pattern is complicated by more bands of rising and falling air, by the way the Earth spins, and by the way the air masses swirl together to create weather systems.

The sky from space
Rising air often makes clouds form, and these can show how the air is moving. The clouds map out the weather systems that can be seen from space, as in this picture taken from the orbiting Space Shuttle.

RISING AND FALLING AIR

In the troposphere, the lowest level of the atmosphere, air rises and falls in a pattern of convection cells called the Hadley, Ferrel, and polar cells. Warm air rising near the equator sinks over the subtropical deserts. Some of the sinking air flows away from the tropics near ground level, rises again, then sinks at the poles.

Warm, moist air rises over the rainforest zone and moves away from the equator.

High-level air flows south, in the Hadley cell. North of the equator, the air flows north.

The air sinks in the subtropics, and some flows south at low level in the southern Ferrel cell.

In the far south, cold air sinks over Antarctica and then flows north in the southern polar cell.

THE CORIOLIS EFFECT

As the Earth spins on its axis, it makes moving air masses swerve off course. Instead of heading north or south, the moving air is pushed to the right in the northern hemisphere, and to the left in the southern hemisphere. This is the Coriolis effect. It creates prevailing winds, such as the trade winds that always blow towards the west over tropical oceans. The prevailing winds carry weather systems with them, and this is why the weather usually comes from the same direction.

Direction of spin

Air moving off course

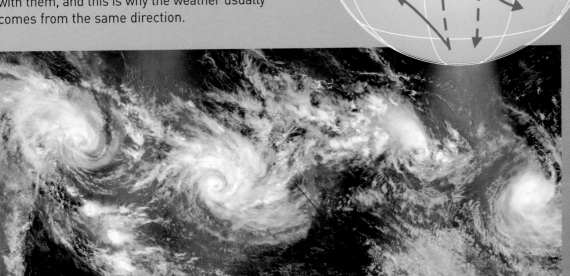

Swirling cyclones ▲
The Coriolis effect also makes local winds swerve off course. These winds blow into regions where warm air is rising. But instead of blowing straight into these regions, the winds veer to one side, then circle around like these tropical cyclones in the Indian Ocean.

The swirling clouds are carried by winds that spiral into each cyclone and then spill out of the top.

Storm clouds rise high into the air, to the bottom of the stratosphere.

The world's weather is powered by the heat of the Sun. This is strongest in tropical regions near the equator, where the Sun's rays are more concentrated. Near the North and South poles the Sun's rays are spread out, so they do not heat the Earth so strongly. This makes these regions much cooler than the tropics. You can see how this works using a torch and a balloon.

WHAT YOU WILL NEED

- Large round balloon (any colour)
- Black marker or felt-tip pen
- Torch (for the best results, use a torch with a beam that can be focused)

1 **Blow up the** balloon, and ask an adult to tie the neck. Use the marker or felt-tip pen to draw a line around the middle. This represents the Earth's equator.

HANDY TIP

Try to keep the torch at about the same distance from the balloon as you move it upwards.

Focus the torch so the beam is as narrow as possible

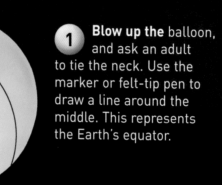

TROPICAL DESERTS

The intense sunlight in the tropics makes them very hot. In dry areas this leads to the formation of hot deserts of bare rock and sand, where few plants can grow. In wet regions the heat helps to form huge clouds, which spill tropical rain onto warm rainforests.

2 **Darken the room** a little, and ask someone to hold the balloon with the equator horizontal. Aim the torch directly at the equator, to make a bright, circular patch of light.

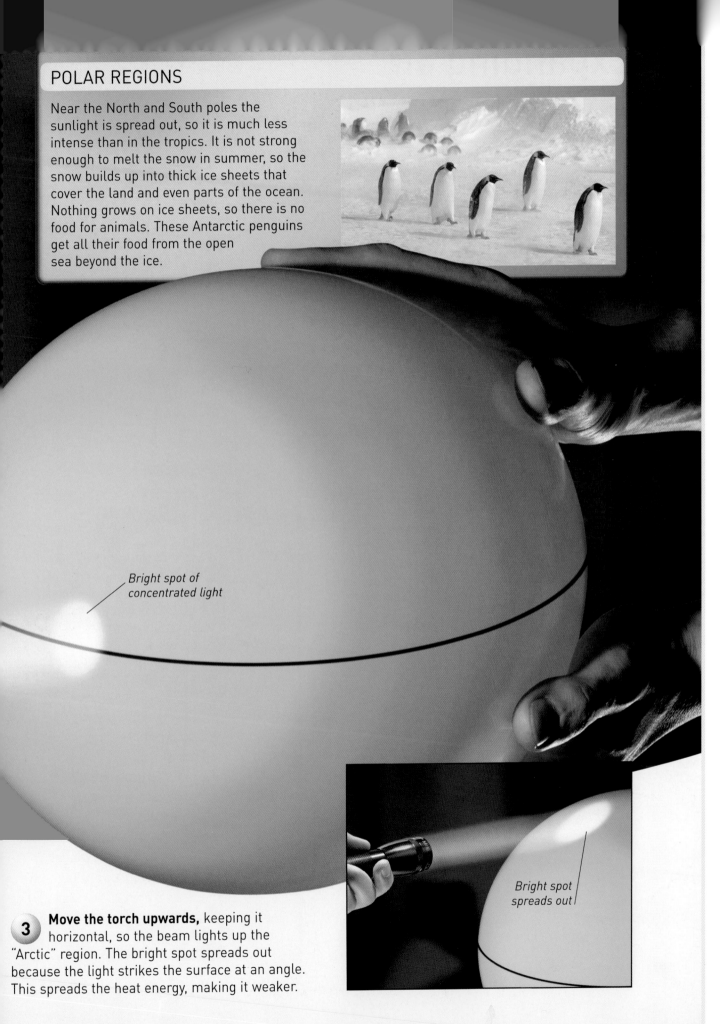

POLAR REGIONS

Near the North and South poles the sunlight is spread out, so it is much less intense than in the tropics. It is not strong enough to melt the snow in summer, so the snow builds up into thick ice sheets that cover the land and even parts of the ocean. Nothing grows on ice sheets, so there is no food for animals. These Antarctic penguins get all their food from the open sea beyond the ice.

*Bright spot of
concentrated light*

*Bright spot
spreads out*

3 **Move the torch upwards,** keeping it horizontal, so the beam lights up the "Arctic" region. The bright spot spreads out because the light strikes the surface at an angle. This spreads the heat energy, making it weaker.

Expanding air

The Sun heats the continents and oceans, especially in tropical regions. Heat rising off the warm ground and sea warms up the air in the lower atmosphere, and this makes it grow in volume, or expand. Expanding warm air usually floats upwards, carrying moisture with it. This air movement leads to the formation of clouds, and powers the world's weather. You can show how warm air expands by using hot water to power a bottle fountain.

MOVING MOLECULES

Air is made of gas particles, or molecules. Heating the molecules gives them more energy. The energy makes them move about more, so they need more space. They move apart, so they take up more room. This makes warm air expand. If the air is cooled again, the air molecules lose energy and move closer together, so cooled air contracts.

Cold molecules move less and take up less space

Warm molecules move more and take up more space

Heat and motion ▲
Heat is a form of energy. When an air molecule is heated, some of the heat energy is turned into motion. So warm air molecules move about more than cold ones, and move further apart.

1 **Place the pebbles** in the bottle and then, using the funnel, half-fill it with cold water. Add a few drops of food colouring to the water. Dry the neck of the bottle if it is wet.

2 **Place the straw** in the bottle, making sure the bottom end is well underwater. Seal the straw in place by fixing a ball of putty around the straw at the neck of the bottle.

WHAT YOU WILL NEED

• Small plastic bottle
• Some pebbles
• Funnel
• Cold and boiling water
• Food colouring
• Sticky putty
• Drinking straw
• Needle or safety pin
• Large heatproof jug

Ask for adult help with the pin and boiling water.

THERMOMETER

You can see how heat makes things expand by watching a thermometer. The liquid in a thermometer expands when it gets warmer, making the liquid rise up the tube. When the temperature falls, the liquid contracts and sinks back down again. The liquid expands at a fixed rate as its temperature goes up, so the height it reaches in the tube gives an accurate measure of temperature.

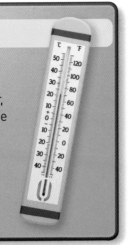

The water may spray up to 40 cm (16 in) into the air

HANDY TIP

The smaller the hole in the plug of putty, the higher the jet will squirt. Stand back!

Make sure the seal around the straw is airtight

3 **Plug the end** of the straw with another piece of putty. Pierce this plug with the needle or pin to make a tiny hole.

4 **Pour boiling** water into the heatproof jug. You need enough to cover most of the bottle. Carefully place the bottle into the hot water. The heat will make the air in the bottle expand, pushing coloured water up the straw and squirting it into the air.

IMPORTANT

Be very careful with food dye as it stains everything. It's best to do this experiment in the kitchen sink, and mop up any spills straight away.

WHAT YOU WILL NEED

- Small cup
- Hot and cold water
- Food colouring
- Cling film
- Rubber band
- Large glass jar with wide mouth
- Long, sharp kitchen knife or skewer

Ask an adult to help when using the hot water and the knife.

Rising warm air

When warm air expands, its gas particles move apart, so the air is less dense. This makes it lighter than cool air. The lighter warm air rises through the heavier cool air in a convection current, or thermal. Air is invisible, so you can't see this happening. But since water behaves in the same way, you can make a thermal using hot and cold water and some food colouring.

1 **Fill the cup** to the brim with hot water, and add some food colouring. Cut a circle of cling film and spread it over the top of the cup. Stretch the rubber band over the film to hold it in place.

2 **Carefully put the cup** of hot, coloured water in the bottom of the glass jar. The cling film should stop it from spilling. Then gradually fill the jar with cold water, almost to the top.

3 **Cut the cling film** with the sharp point of the knife or skewer. You need a single, fairly large gash. Then take the knife out and watch as the warm, coloured water starts to appear through the gash.

AIR POWER

Hot air balloons are filled with ordinary air that is heated up with a gas burner. As the air is heated it expands, becoming less dense and lighter than the cool air outside the balloon. This makes it float upwards, carrying the balloon with it. Thermals of warm air rise through colder air in the same way, but you can't see them because the air itself is invisible.

◄ **Extra heat**
The balloon is held up by hot air, not by gas from the gas burner. It starts to sink as the air cools, so the pilot has to fire up the gas for a few seconds to warm it up again.

WARM AIR CURRENTS

If you blow bubbles across the top of a warm radiator or electric heater, they will be caught up in the rising currents of warm air – thermals – and float up with them. Soaring birds, such as eagles, float upwards on thermals in the same way, circling in the rising warm air to gain height.

The coloured water slowly cools and sinks

4 **A plume of** hot water will rise through the cold surrounding water and float above it, just like a thermal of warm air.

5 **If you leave** the cup and jar for long enough, the warm, coloured water at the surface will cool down. As it cools it becomes more dense and heavy, and starts to sink towards the bottom of the jar. Cool air sinks in the same way.

HANDY TIP

Put the cup in the kitchen sink while you are filling it with hot water and covering it with cling film.

WHAT YOU WILL NEED

- Wide-neck jar or bowl
- Large balloon
- Scissors
- Sticky tape
- 2 drinking straws
- Coloured card
- Marker pen
- Ruler

Measure air pressure

When warm air expands and rises, it reduces the weight and pressure of air on the ground below. This creates what weather forecasters call a low-pressure zone – an area of warm, light air. Cool air is heavier, so it sinks and puts more pressure on the ground below, creating a high-pressure zone. Pressure changes show how weather is changing and moving. You can measure them using a home-made barometer.

1 **Cut the neck** off the balloon, together with part of its body. You should have just over half the balloon left. Stretch this tightly over the top of the bowl as if you are making a drum. Tape the balloon in place.

High air pressure pushes the balloon down, moving the pointer

2 **Make a short slit** in the end of one straw and push this end inside the other straw. Tape them together. Tape one end of the extra-long straw to the middle of the balloon, so it rests on the rim of the bowl.

3 **Fold the card** so it stands upright. Use the pen and ruler to mark a scale on it, with the lines 6 mm (¼ in) apart.

The straw pointer will drop if the air pressure falls

MAPPING AIR PRESSURE

Isobar

Barometers are used to measure air pressure at many different locations. The pressures are marked on maps, and any pressures that are the same are linked with lines called isobars. The result is a map of pressure zones, with areas of high and low pressure marked by the isobars. These highs and lows indicate what the weather is like on the ground.

4 **Put the bowl** on a shelf where it will not be disturbed, and stand the scale by the pointer.

If air pressure rises, the pointer will move up

5 **Check the** barometer every few hours to see if the pointer has moved up or down to show a change in air pressure.

High and low pressure

Weather forecasters can work out what the weather is like simply by looking at maps of pressure zones. Where warm air is rising, causing low pressure, it often creates clouds and rain. Where cool air is sinking, causing high pressure, it often creates clear, sunny skies. The wind blows from high-pressure zones to low-pressure zones, so forecasters can work out wind directions, and also how strong the wind might be. The pressure zones usually move from day to day, taking their weather with them.

Low-pressure weather ▲
Rising warm air in low-pressure zones carries moisture up into the sky with it. The air cools as it rises higher, and this makes clouds form. Tiny water droplets inside the clouds come together to form big drops that may fall as rain. This is why low-pressure weather is usually cloudy and rainy, with grey skies that block out the sunshine.

High-pressure weather ▲
Sinking cool air in high-pressure zones stops moisture rising into the sky. This prevents clouds from forming, so there is no rain. The sky is blue, and summer high-pressure weather is sunny and warm. High-pressure weather in winter can be sunny too, but at night there is no cloud to stop heat escaping into space, so it can also get very cold.

Creating a breeze

Air flows away from high-pressure zones, where cool air is sinking, towards low-pressure zones, where warm air is rising. This creates wind. Some winds blow over great distances, but others, such as sea breezes, are local. Using ice and hot sand, you can see how a breeze works by observing how smoke is blown from a tiny high-pressure zone to a tiny low-pressure zone.

THE SEA BREEZE

On warm summer days the land heats up more quickly than the sea. It warms the air above and causes it to rise. Cooler air from above the sea is drawn towards land, creating a sea breeze. Meanwhile, warm air flows out to sea at a high level. This cools and sinks to replace the air that has blown onshore.

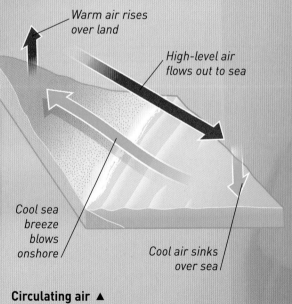

Warm air rises over land

High-level air flows out to sea

Cool sea breeze blows onshore

Cool air sinks over sea

Circulating air ▲
Rising warm air over the land forms a small low-pressure zone. Sinking cool air over the sea forms a small high-pressure zone. Since air flows from high to low pressure, this creates a breeze.

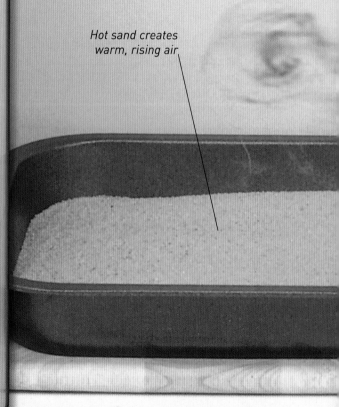

Hot sand creates warm, rising air

1 **Fill one tray** with sand, and ask an adult to place it in the oven on low heat to warm up.

2 **Use the scissors** to cut the front off the cardboard box – the box acts as a screen to block out draughts. Put the mats in the bottom of the box.

3 **Fill the second** baking tray with ice from the freezer, and put it on one of the mats. Ask your adult helper to take the warm tray from the oven and place it on the other mat, so the two trays are side by side.

4 **Light an incense stick** and hold it between the two trays. As the warm air rises off the warm tray it creates a low-pressure zone. The smoke will be blown towards the warm tray from the high-pressure zone above the cold tray.

TRADE WINDS

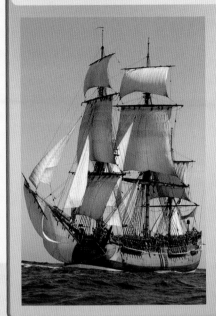

In tropical oceans, hot sunshine near the equator makes warm air rise high into the atmosphere. The rising air is replaced by air blowing in over the sea from subtropical regions, where cool air is sinking. This giant version of a sea breeze creates the trade winds.

◄ Power supply for ships
In the past, sailing ships relied on the steady, predictable trade winds to carry them across the oceans.

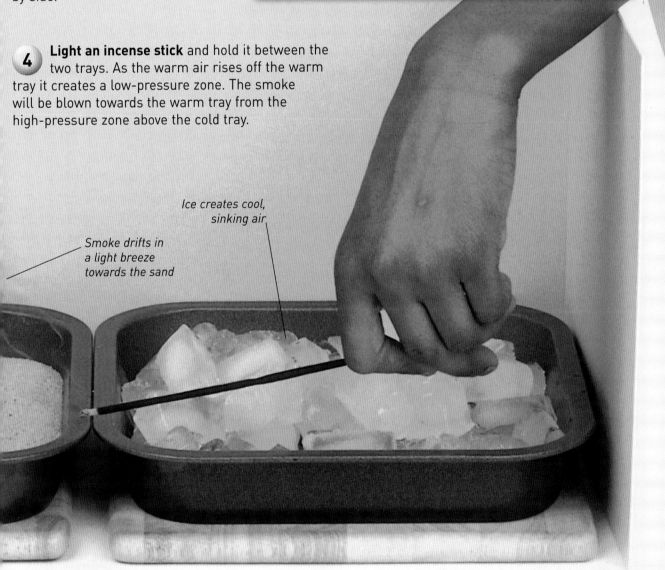

Smoke drifts in a light breeze towards the sand

Ice creates cool, sinking air

Make a wind vane

The wind doesn't blow straight from high-pressure zones to low-pressure zones. It spirals around them, like water swirling down a drain. So when a moving low-pressure system is approaching, the wind changes. As it passes overhead, the wind keeps changing, then finally settles when the weather system has moved on. You can watch for these shifts using a wind vane.

WHAT YOU WILL NEED

- A4 sheet of stiff card
- Pencil
- Scissors
- 2 small coins
- Pen top
- Sticky tape
- Kitchen or barbecue skewer
- Long garden cane
- 4 clothes pegs (1 a different colour)
- Compass

Ask an adult to help when using the skewer.

1 **Score down** the centre of a piece of stiff card and fold it in two. Draw two diagonal lines from the bottom corners of the card to the top of the central fold. Cut along the lines to make a long folded triangle.

2 **Tape two** small coins inside the triangle, on one side near the tip. The weight of the coins will help balance the wind vane when it is finished.

3 **Fold the triangle** together and tape it up. Balance the triangle on a pencil and make a mark at the balance point. Tape the pen top to the card at the mark. This will form the pivot of the wind vane.

INTO THE WIND

When light aircraft take off they head into the wind, because this lifts them off the runway quicker. That is why small airfields have wind indicators. The runway is usually built so it faces the prevailing wind, but if the wind changes dramatically the aircraft may have to take off from the other end.

◄ **Windsock**
Airfields use windsocks as wind indicators. They show the strength of the wind as well as its direction.

MOVING WEATHER SYSTEMS

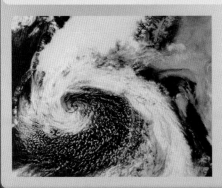

Satellite images of moving weather systems show how the wind swirls around them in giant spirals, carrying cloud with it. As different parts of the spiral system move overhead, the wind at ground level keeps changing direction.

◀ **Low-pressure spiral**
This low-pressure system in the northern hemisphere is swirling anticlockwise and moving from west to east. The wind keeps changing as the low-pressure system approaches and passes overhead.

HANDY TIP

Site the vane well away from buildings or trees that could interfere with the wind.

5 **Put the vane** on the skewer and make sure it spins freely. Push the cane into soft ground or tie it to a post. Using a compass, turn the cane so the coloured peg points north.

4 **Tape the skewer** to a long garden cane, with the pointed end at the top. Attach the four clothes pegs to the cane in a cross, near the top.

6 **The vane points** towards the direction from which the wind is blowing. Note the wind direction over a week or two. Does it usually blow from one direction? This is the prevailing wind, which blows unless upset by a moving weather system.

N

The red peg indicates north

Measure wind speed

Air is squeezed out of high-pressure zones and flows to nearby low-pressure zones. This creates the wind. A big difference in air pressure between the two zones makes the wind blow faster. If the two zones move closer together, this also increases the wind speed, and the faster the wind blows, the stronger it is. Wind speed is measured using an instrument called an anemometer. You can make your own simple version using four paper cups.

1 **Mark one** of the paper cups by sticking coloured tape around the outside.

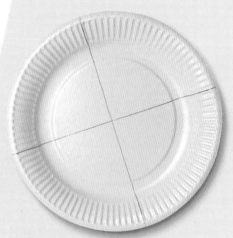

2 **Using the pencil**, draw a cross on the plate to find the centre. This will be the pivot point for the anemometer.

WEATHER MAPS

The isobar lines on a weather map surround zones of high or low pressure. Each line marks a different level of air pressure. In some places lines are close together, while in other places they are further apart. The closer they are, the steeper the pressure difference between the high-pressure and low-pressure zones, and the stronger the wind.

Mapping the wind ▲
On this weather map of Europe, the tight isobars over northern France show that it is very windy there. The widely spaced isobars over Sweden show that the wind is light. The wind blows along the isobars, around the pressure centres.

3 **Stick a short length** of double-sided tape to the side of each cup. Attach one cup to the nearest edge of the paper plate, so its open end is on the left. Turn the plate and attach the other cups in the same way.

WHAT YOU WILL NEED

- Paper plate
- 4 paper cups
- Coloured tape
- Pinboard pin with plastic end
- Eraser-tipped pencil
- Double-sided tape
- Stopwatch

Ask an adult to help with the pin.

A PROFESSIONAL ANEMOMETER

The anemometers used in weather stations are similar to the home-made version. The main difference is that the spinning cups are linked to an electronic device that counts the turns, and converts them into a display of the wind speed.

Speed and direction ▶
This anemometer is mounted above a wind vane, to show the wind direction as well as the wind speed.

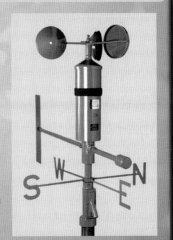

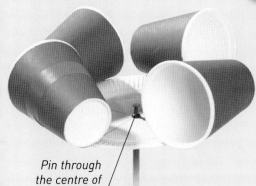

Pin through the centre of the plate

4 **Pin the plate** to the eraser on the end of the pencil, so that the pin passes through the centre of the cross. Hold the anemometer up so it spins in the wind.

5 **Using the stopwatch**, count how often the marked cup passes round in 30 seconds. Write down the number next to the local wind speed, which you can find on a website. Do this for several days and make a chart in which you translate the numbers into wind speeds.

Watch the marked cup and count how many times it spins in the wind

Invisible water

Water that is warmed by the Sun turns to water vapour, a gas that is carried upwards by rising warm air. It is invisible, unlike steam, and it forms at quite low temperatures. Huge masses of water vapour rise off tropical oceans, which have surface temperatures of about 20°C (68°F). This is the level at which your central heating is likely to be set. Try creating water vapour at home using a radiator.

WHAT YOU WILL NEED

- Large glass jar
- Cool water
- Cool glass bowl with curved base that will sit in the mouth of the jar
- Warm place, such as the top of a radiator or the warm vent at the back of a refrigerator

HUMIDITY

The amount of water vapour in the air is referred to as its humidity. Warm air can hold more water vapour than cold air. This means that warm, wet places are very humid, creating that tropical, sticky feeling.

Hygrometer ▶
Humidity is measured with a hygrometer, which uses a modified thermometer to detect water vapour in the air.

Condensation

When it is cold outside and warm inside, the low temperature of a window can cause water vapour in the warm air to turn back into water. Droplets form on the inside of the window in a process called condensation. It is the opposite of evaporation, which turns liquid water into vapour.

EVAPORATION

The water of oceans and lakes is always turning to water vapour. The process is called evaporation. It also happens on land, and this is why wet things dry out in hot sunshine. As the water turns to vapour it leaves everything else behind, including any substances such as salt that were dissolved in the water.

◄ Salt Lake

In deserts, lakes form like giant puddles after rare rainstorms, and then dry out in the desert heat. As the water evaporates it leaves any dissolved salt behind, so the remaining water gets more and more salty. White salt crystals form on rocks on the lake shores, like these at the edges of the Great Salt Lake in Utah, USA.

1 **Put some** cool water into the glass jar. A depth of about 5 cm (2 in) is plenty.

Water droplets on the bottom of the glass bowl

2 **Stand the jar** in a warm place. Put the cool glass bowl on top, so the base of the bowl seals the mouth of the jar.

3 **Over time,** water droplets appear on the bottom of the glass bowl. Water is evaporating in the jar, and then condensing on the cool base of the bowl to form liquid water again. The water vapour itself is invisible.

HANDY TIP

Put the glass bowl in the refrigerator to cool it down before placing it on the jar.

Morning dew

On cool, clear nights, heat from the ground escapes into the sky. If the ground gets cold enough, water vapour in the air above it is cooled to below the temperature where it turns to liquid water. This condenses on the cool grass as dew. You can try two experiments to gather your own dew.

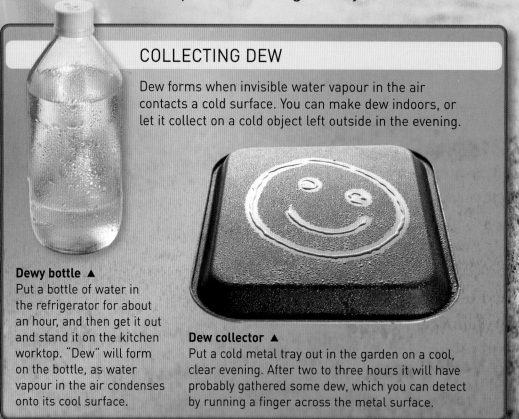

COLLECTING DEW

Dew forms when invisible water vapour in the air contacts a cold surface. You can make dew indoors, or let it collect on a cold object left outside in the evening.

Dewy bottle ▲
Put a bottle of water in the refrigerator for about an hour, and then get it out and stand it on the kitchen worktop. "Dew" will form on the bottle, as water vapour in the air condenses onto its cool surface.

Dew collector ▲
Put a cold metal tray out in the garden on a cool, clear evening. After two to three hours it will have probably gathered some dew, which you can detect by running a finger across the metal surface.

Life-giving dew

In places where it rarely rains and water is scarce, dew is a vital source of moisture for plants and animals. Many desert plants rely on dew, and have special systems for collecting it. All over the world, animals that dry out easily are most active on nights when the grass is covered in dew.

Frog ▼
Thin-skinned frogs emerge from pools to hunt on land at night. Dew keeps their skin damp and stops their bodies from drying out.

Welwitschia plant ▲
In the Namib Desert of southwest Africa, the odd-looking welwitschia plant gathers dew through its extremely long, ragged leaves.

Footprints in the dew

On grass, dew forms small drops of water that reflect the light. When someone walks across the grass the reflective drops are scattered, so the footprints look darker.

CLEAR SKIES

Dew is most likely to form on bright moonlit or starry nights. The Moon and stars are visible because there is no cloud to hide them. Thick cloud acts like a blanket, stopping heat escaping into space, so the ground may not get cool enough to condense airborne water vapour into dew.

Full Moon ▲

The sky gets clearer at the end of summer when temperatures fall and there is less water vapour in the air. You can see more details on the Moon and more stars. Meanwhile, dew collecting on spiders' webs makes them stretch as the silk absorbs water.

◄ Darkling beetle

Another resident of the Namib Desert is this beetle. It collects dew on its body at night, then raises its tail end so the dew trickles down into its mouth.

◄ Air plants

In the tropics, instead of growing in soil, many plants grow on rainforest trees. They get all the water they need from water vapour in the air condensing on their leaves.

Winter frost

The soft white hoar frost that forms on plants, fences, and windows in winter is dew that has settled on freezing cold objects and turned into ice crystals. The water vapour in the air turns directly to ice, without passing through the liquid water phase. You can see this happening by using ice cubes and salt to make your own frost.

1 **Fill the glass** with ice and add some salt. The salt makes the ice melt, and when it does this it draws in heat from the surrounding air. This lowers the air temperature and cools the glass.

BLACK ICE

Very cold rain falling on freezing cold roads at night can form glassy sheets of ice called glaze. It is often referred to as black ice because you can see the dark colour of the road through the ice. Since it looks like water and is very slippery, black ice is far more dangerous than hoar frost or even snow. It causes a lot of accidents in winter.

Melting the ice ▲
In northern countries where black ice is a regular problem, special mobile heaters are used to melt it and make the roads safer.

2 **Frost crystals** grow on the outside of the chilled glass, just like hoar frost forming on an ice-cold leaf. The crystals have formed from invisible water vapour in the air, which turns directly to ice when it contacts the glass.

STEAMING FROST

Frost often forms on clear, cold winter nights. If the sky is still clear in the morning, the warm sunshine can turn the ice straight back into water vapour. This is hoar frost formation in reverse.

Sublimation ▲
As frost turns to water vapour in the morning sunshine, it often looks like steam rising off the trees. This process of ice turning to vapour without becoming liquid water first is called sublimation.

Frost and ice

The frost that forms on cold objects in winter can be very beautiful, creating wonderful feathery patterns of ice crystals. But thick layers of ice can add so much weight to trees and cables that they sometimes collapse under the strain.

Frost patterns ▶
If dew forms on a smooth surface, such as glass, and then freezes, it forms leafy, fern-like patterns as the ice crystals grow.

Hoar frost ▶
When water vapour freezes onto leaves, the first ice crystals form at the edges, which are the coldest parts of the leaf.

Rime ▶
Water droplets in very cold freezing fog can freeze onto cold objects, forming thick layers of white ice crystals called rime.

Heavy ice ▶
Power lines can become thickly covered in rime, glaze, or hanging icicles. These can be so heavy that they cause the lines to snap.

Ice storms ▶
Places such as Canada sometimes suffer ice storms of heavy glaze that can break tree branches.

Clouds and fog

As warm air rises, it cools, and any water vapour in the rising air cools, too. Eventually, it gets cool enough to condense into the tiny droplets of water that form clouds. But the vapour needs something to condense onto, such as microscopic dust or smoke particles in the air, called condensation nuclei. These allow cooled water vapour to turn into clouds. You can show how this works using warm water, ice, and smoke particles from a smouldering match.

1 **Tape the black paper** or card to the back of the jar to create a dark background. This will make your cloud more visible. Fill around a third of the jar with warm (but not steaming) water.

2 **Light a match,** and then blow it out. Wait for a second or two before dropping the smoking match into the jar. Quickly put the bag of ice on top of the jar, so it forms a cold lid over the opening.

FOG

If water vapour in the air condenses into cloud droplets at ground level, it forms the low-lying clouds we call fog. This often happens on cold, clear nights when the ground cools down quickly, cooling the air above it so any water vapour condenses into radiation fog. It also happens at sea when warm, moist air moves over cold water, cooling the vapour so it turns into sea fog.

Pacific coast fog ▲
Off the coast of California, USA, moist air is cooled by the cold Californian current that flows south from Alaska. Water vapour condenses into sea fogs that roll in under the Golden Gate Bridge in San Francisco.

WHAT YOU WILL NEED

- Large, wide-necked glass jar
- Warm water
- Black paper or card
- Sticky tape
- Plastic sandwich bag filled with ice cubes
- Matches

 Ask for adult help with the match.

3 **Water vapour** rising from the warm water condenses onto the smoke particles and forms a cloud. Lifting off the ice bag releases the cloud.

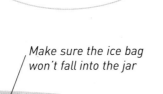
HANDY TIP
Don't drop the match in too quickly after blowing it out, or you'll get too much smoke.

Make sure the ice bag won't fall into the jar

Birth of a cloud

Clouds seem to form out of nothing, because the water vapour that becomes cloud droplets is an invisible gas. Cloud droplets are so tiny that it takes a million of them to form a raindrop, but they are big enough to be visible.

Cloud droplets form ▶
Invisible water vapour carried upwards in warm air currents gets cooler as it rises. As it cools, the water vapour starts to form cloud droplets around microscopic condensation nuclei.

White haze ▶
As more cloud droplets form, the young cloud starts to become visible as white haze or wisps of white against the blue sky.

Floating water ▶
The cloud droplets are so tiny that they are able to float on the rising air currents even though they are made of liquid water.

White and grey ▶
The cloud becomes thick enough to stop the sunlight shining through it, so the thickest parts are in shadow and appear grey.

Clouds and rain ▶
Eventually, the cloud droplets may join together to make much bigger, heavier water drops, and these then fall as rain.

Watching the clouds

Clouds form as warm, moist air rises and cools. This makes the invisible water vapour in the air turn into tiny water droplets or ice crystals. There are three main reasons why the air rises. Areas of land or sea warmed by the Sun can warm the air above them, making it expand and rise into the sky by convection. A warm air mass can be forced upwards by colder, heavier air pushing beneath it. Air can also be pushed upwards as it flows over hills and mountains.

Convection clouds

Big storm clouds often form when moist air is heated by the warm ground below. The warm air rises and cools, forming a cloud. As the cloud forms, however, some energy is released, which warms the air a little more. This makes it rise a bit higher, forming more cloud, so it grows upwards. If there is enough moisture in the air, the cloud can grow to the bottom of the stratosphere, and may be more than 10 km (6 miles) high. These are called cumulonimbus clouds.

The cloud is built up by heat released from inside the cloud itself

PHOTOGRAPHING CLOUDS

You can use a camera to help you study clouds. Whenever you see an interesting cloud, take a photograph of it. Then try to identify it using a book on cloud types. You can also find information on clouds on the Internet. Gradually, you will build up a collection. As you identify the clouds you have photographed, you will discover new clouds to look for.

When it cannot rise any higher, the top of the cloud spreads sideways in a veil of tiny ice crystals _____

Main types of cloud

There are three main types of clouds. Each has a Latin name that describes its form: cirrus (wispy), cumulus (heaped), or stratus (sheet). These names are used together to describe other clouds such as cirrostratus (wispy sheets of high-level cloud).

CLOUD WAVE

If moist air is pushed up a mountain, it cools and the water vapour turns into a cloud above the peak. Often the air warms up as it sinks on the other side, so although cloud keeps forming above the mountain, it soon turns to vapour again. The result is a cloud that seems to sit on the mountain top.

Cloud-topped mountain ▲
Air passing over the snow-capped peak of Tungurahua in Ecuador, South America, is forming a wave-shaped cloud. The wave is rising above the peak, cooling the air and turning invisible water vapour into cloud droplets. On the right, however, the air is sinking and warming, and this is making the cloud droplets evaporate.

Cirrus ▶
Clouds that always form high in the sky (where the air is very cold) are known as cirrus clouds. These thin, wispy-looking clouds are made of ice crystals, and often form long trails.

Cumulus ▶
These fluffy white clouds often form in good weather as warm air rises into the cool blue sky. They can, however, grow into giant cumulonimbus clouds (nimbus means rain).

Stratus ▶
Flat sheets of stratus cloud form at low level in the centres of low-pressure weather systems, or depressions. They make the sky grey, but do not usually bring rain.

Weather fronts

When warm air flowing from the tropics meets cold air from nearer the poles, the warm air rises above the cold air. As it rises it cools, resulting in clouds and rain. The boundary between the two air masses is called a front. It is invisible in air, but you can create a "front" between warm and cold water, using food colouring to show the separate layers.

WHAT YOU WILL NEED

- Large glass jar
- Jug
- Very hot water (but not boiling)
- Very cold water
- Food colouring
- Thermometer

Ask for adult help when using the hot water.

The warm, coloured water stays at the top

1 **Fill the jug** with the hot water and add some of the food colouring. Pour the cold water into the big jar so it is more than half full.

2 **Tip the jar** of cold water so the water is close to the rim. Very slowly and gently, pour the hot coloured water from the jug down the neck of the jar, so it trickles into the cold water. The coloured water should stay near the surface.

A WARM FRONT

When warm air pushes against cold air, the warm air rides up over the cold air at a shallow angle. The angled boundary between the air masses is known as a warm front. Steeper boundaries caused by cold air pushing beneath warm air are called cold fronts.

Warm air rides up over cold air

Rising warm air ▶
As the warm air slides up and over the cold air at the front, it gets cooler. This makes water vapour in the air turn to clouds and rain.

3 **If you get** it right, the warm, coloured water will lie in a layer above the heavier cold water, just as warm air lies above cold air. The boundary between the two is like a weather front. You can test the difference in temperature using a thermometer.

Dip the thermometer below the "front" and see the temperature fall

▲ Moving frontier
The winds blow mainly towards the east around the polar front, carrying the weather systems with them. The shape of the front changes all the time, and it is often broken up into separate fronts.

THE POLAR FRONT

Some types of front affect the weather over huge areas. The polar front forms where warm tropical air meets cold polar air over North America, Europe, and northern Asia. It makes a wavy line around the globe where the warm and cold air masses push into each other. The waves in the polar front cause the mobile weather systems that make the weather so variable in these northern regions.

Swirling air

When a warm air mass rises over a cold air mass at a front, the rising air reduces the air pressure on the ground below. The pressure is lowest where the air is rising quickest. The surrounding air swirls into this low-pressure area and is sucked upwards. The warm and cold air masses swirl around each other too, separated by warm and cold fronts that bring clouds and rain as they pass overhead. This type of low-pressure weather system is called a a cyclone, a depression, or simply a low.

Cloudy weather

The rising warm air in a low-pressure weather system usually creates a lot of cloud. Huge banks of cloud can build up over the weather fronts that separate the warm and cold air masses. They often produce a lot of rain, and big clouds over cold fronts sometimes cause thunderstorms.

ATLANTIC CYCLONE

Cyclones are very common over the north Atlantic, where warm tropical air meets cold polar air at the polar front. The cyclones push eastwards, carrying cloudy, rainy weather over northern Europe. They are marked by spirals of cloud that can be seen from space. Orbiting weather satellites send images of them back to Earth.

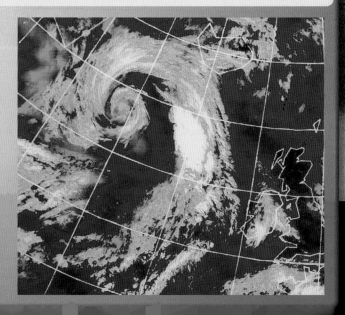

Cloud spiral ▶
This false colour satellite image shows an Atlantic cyclone approaching Britain and Iceland. As with all low-pressure systems in the northern hemisphere, it is spiralling anticlockwise.

SWIRLING CYCLONE

If you watch water draining down a plughole you will get a good idea of how air is drawn into a cyclone – but remember that the air rises at the centre instead of sinking. The spinning Earth makes cyclones swirl anticlockwise north of the equator, but clockwise south of the equator. They are balanced by anticyclones, which swirl down and outwards in the opposite direction.

Down the drain ▲
Air swirls into a cyclone rather like water pouring down a drain. It circles in a vortex rather than flowing straight into the centre.

The life of a cyclone

Temperate northern cyclones normally move from west to east, developing as they go. Warm and cold air masses twist around each other, forcing warm moist air upwards and generating high winds, clouds, and rain.

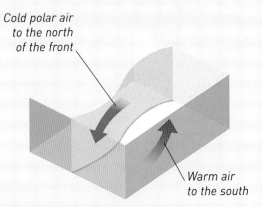

Cold polar air to the north of the front

Warm air to the south

Air masses twist around ▲
A Northern Hemisphere cyclone begins with a mass of warm air pushing north, to the right of a mass of cold air. They are separated by a front.

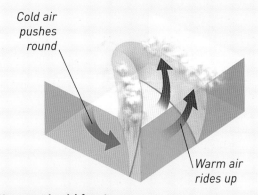

Cold air pushes round

Warm air rides up

Warm and cold fronts ▲
The warm air rides up over cold air to the east, at a warm front. Meanwhile, cold air from the west pushes the warm air up at a cold front. Both fronts are marked by clouds and rain.

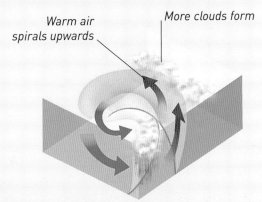

Warm air spirals upwards

More clouds form

Cyclone occludes ▲
The cold air from the west moves faster than the warm air, pushes under it, and lifts it right off the ground. This is called an occlusion.

Track a cyclone

A moving low-pressure weather system, or cyclone, has a warm front and a cold front, with warm air in the middle that is pushed up to form clouds. There are different types of clouds at the warm and cold fronts. By identifying them as they pass over, and checking changes in air pressure and wind direction, you can track the progress of a cyclone.

Moving weather

In the diagram of the cyclone shown below, the cyclone is moving from west to east. At the centre is a zone of warm air. At its leading edge, warm air is sliding up over cold air at the warm front. The rising air forms a sequence of clouds, from high-level cirrus to low-level nimbostratus. As the cyclone passes over, cold air from behind forces warm air up at the cold front, forming big cumulonimbus clouds.

ⓐ Cumulus clouds Small cumulus clouds often follow the cold front, causing showers. Eventually, they blow away and the sky clears.

ⓑ Cumulonimbus clouds A narrow band of cumulonimbus clouds can form over the cold front, causing heavy rain.

ⓒ Stratus clouds Flat, low-level stratus clouds often cover the sky in the middle of the moving cyclone. The weather is dull, but not rainy.

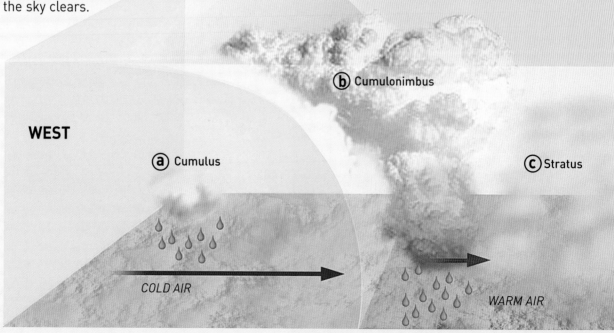

WEST

ⓐ Cumulus

ⓑ Cumulonimbus

ⓒ Stratus

COLD AIR

WARM AIR

Cold front ▲

PRESSURE AND WIND

As a cyclone passes over, the air pressure and wind direction change. You can use your home-made barometer and wind vane to keep track of these changes. The pressure falls as clouds build up over the warm front, and keeps falling. Meanwhile, the wind swings around to blow from a different direction, which varies depending on where you are. As the warm front passes, the pressure stays low, but the wind often changes back to how it was. As the cold front passes, the pressure rises again.

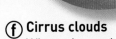

ⓓ Nimbostratus clouds
Thick, grey, low-level nimbostratus clouds build up over the warm front. As they pass over they bring steady rain.

ⓔ Altostratus clouds
Thin cirrostratus and cirrus become thicker, lower altostratus as the warm front gets nearer, and the air pressure falls steadily.

ⓕ Cirrus clouds
Wispy cirrus clouds that form very high in the sky are the first sign of the approaching cyclone. They gradually expand into sheets of cirrostratus.

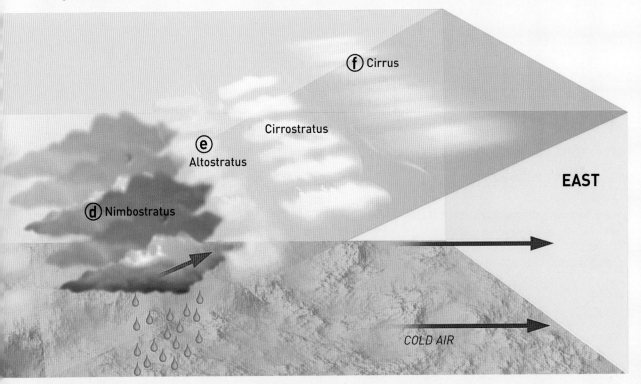

ⓕ Cirrus

Cirrostratus

ⓔ
Altostratus

ⓓ Nimbostratus

EAST

COLD AIR

▲ **Warm front**

Measure rainfall

The tiny water droplets and ice crystals that form clouds may eventually grow into bigger raindrops and snowflakes. When these get heavy enough, they fall towards the ground. The snowflakes often melt on the way, turning into rain. Rainfall is measured in centimetres or inches using a rain gauge, and it is easy to make your own.

WHAT YOU WILL NEED

- Large, clear, straight-sided, plastic bottle
- Coloured tape
- Handful of pebbles
- Scissors
- Ruler
- Water

Ask an adult to help you cut off the bottle top.

1 **Cut the top** off the bottle at the point where the curved "shoulders" join the straight sides. Try to make a straight cut. Save both parts of the bottle (you can throw away the cap).

2 **Put the pebbles** in the bottle. Stick some tape to the side of the bottle above the pebbles. Add water until it reaches the top of the tape.

3 **Turn the top** section of the bottle upside down, and insert it in the lower section of the bottle.

RAIN AND SHOWERS

Rain often falls over quite small areas at a time. Weather forecasters call this type of rain a shower, even though it may be quite heavy. Showers travel across country, so they don't last very long in one place. The steady rainfall caused by broad weather fronts also travels across country, but it extends over such a large area that it can keep falling all day.

Distant rain ▶
You can often see local showers falling in the distance. The rain looks like grey or silver streaks falling from the dark rain clouds.

4 **Put the rain** gauge outside in a place where it is exposed to the sky. If it rains, measure the amount of water above the tape in centimetres or inches. Then pour water out until it is level with the top of the tape again.

The ruler gives an accurate measure of rainfall in centimetres or inches

HANDY TIP

Measure the rainfall every day at the same time to build up a record of annual rainfall.

Make a rainbow

Rainbows are among the most beautiful of all the optical effects created by weather. They are caused by white sunlight passing through falling rain – the raindrops bend the light and split it into all the colours of the spectrum. They are seen only on sunny, showery days, when patchy cloud allows the Sun to shine through the rain. Rainbows always appear opposite the Sun. You can create your own rainbow effect by passing sunlight through a bowl of water.

WHAT YOU WILL NEED

- Shallow dish, such as a plant pot saucer
- Small mirror that will fit inside the dish
- Lump of sticky putty or plasticine
- Sheet of paper
- Low-tack sticky tape

Never look directly at the Sun – it can damage your eyes or blind you.

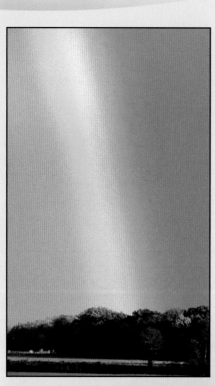

Rainbow colours
A rainbow has violet on the inside of the arc and red on the outside, and every shade of blue, green, yellow, and orange in between. The sky looks darker on the outside of the arc, and sometimes there is a dimmer second rainbow outside the brighter main one, with the colours in reverse order.

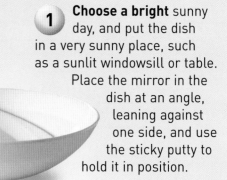

1 **Choose a bright** sunny day, and put the dish in a very sunny place, such as a sunlit windowsill or table. Place the mirror in the dish at an angle, leaning against one side, and use the sticky putty to hold it in position.

HANDY TIP

To avoid spills, fill the dish with water after putting it in the sunny spot.

Use the tape to stick the paper to the wall, or simply hold it up

Your rainbow may be surprisingly vivid

2 **Fill the dish** with water to a depth of about 2.5 cm (1 in), so it covers the lower part of the mirror. Then turn the dish until you see the sunlight reflected onto a nearby wall.

3 **There will be** two patches of light on the wall: an ordinary white reflection from the mirror, and a rainbow reflection that has passed through the water. You may see the rainbow more clearly if you attach the sheet of paper to the wall.

Rotate the dish gently to avoid spills

SPLITTING THE LIGHT

White sunlight is a mixture of all the colours of the rainbow. When a ray of light shines through air or water, such as a raindrop, the light is bent, or refracted. The different colours are bent by different amounts, splitting the ray into a spectrum of rainbow colours. Raindrops split light in the same way, causing a rainbow to form.

Making a spectrum ▶
White light can be bent and split into a spectrum of rainbow colours by shining it through a triangular block of glass called a prism.

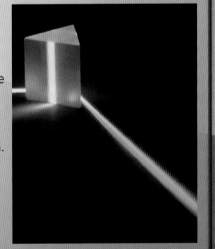

Make a snowflake

When clouds rise high in the sky, their temperature falls below freezing, so the tiny cloud droplets freeze into microscopic ice crystals. These may join together to form snowflakes. Each snowflake contains about 200 ice crystals, in a six-sided pattern. You can see how a snowflake forms by using a substance called borax, which forms beautiful crystals of its own.

WHAT YOU WILL NEED

- Large measuring jug
- 3 white pipe cleaners
- White string
- Scissors • Pencil
- Boiling water
- Borax (sugar or salt can be used as an alternative)
- Wooden spoon
- Blue food colouring

Ask an adult to help you with the boiling water.

CRYSTALLIZATION

The activity on these pages works because cold water cannot dissolve as much borax as hot water. So, as the water cools, solid borax collects on the framework of pipe cleaners and string. As it collects, the borax forms glinting crystals. The slower the water cools down, the bigger the crystals.

Crystal faces flash in the light

Borax crystals ▲
Each crystal is built up from borax molecules that were spread out in the hot water. They clump together in a shape that mirrors their atomic structure.

① Take the three pipe cleaners and twist them together in the centre to make a six-pointed star. Make sure the star is small enough to fit in the jug.

② Tie the string around the points of the star to link them together. The result looks like a snowflake.

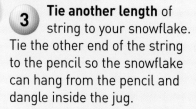

③ Tie another length of string to your snowflake. Tie the other end of the string to the pencil so the snowflake can hang from the pencil and dangle inside the jug.

HANDY TIP

You can buy borax from hardware stores. It should not be ingested.

ICE CRYSTALS

The tiny ice crystals that form high in clouds are shaped like microscopic six-sided rods. They are drawn together by electric forces, along with tiny water droplets. The water freezes and welds the crystals together in an amazing variety of patterns, but since the crystals have six sides, the flakes always have a six-sided or six-pointed form.

◀ **Snowflake variety**
All snowflakes are shaped rather like six-pointed stars, but every one is different because the ice crystals come together in different ways.

Make sure the snowflake is not resting on the bottom of the jug

4 **Pour boiling water** into the jug, and add a spoonful of borax. Using the spoon, stir until the borax is dissolved. Keep adding borax and stirring until no more will dissolve. Add a few drops of blue food colouring.

5 **Hang the snowflake** in the jug so that it is immersed in the liquid. Wait at least overnight, or longer if you are using sugar or salt. The next day, your snowflake will be covered with beautiful crystals.

Storm clouds and hail

The biggest clouds are the black storm clouds known as cumulonimbus clouds. They tower high into the sky, and are much deeper than other clouds. They are made of water droplets at the bottom and ice crystals at the top. Powerful air currents toss the crystals around, making them gather more ice and grow into hailstones. The currents also rub the droplets and crystals against each other, generating static electricity that is eventually discharged as lightning.

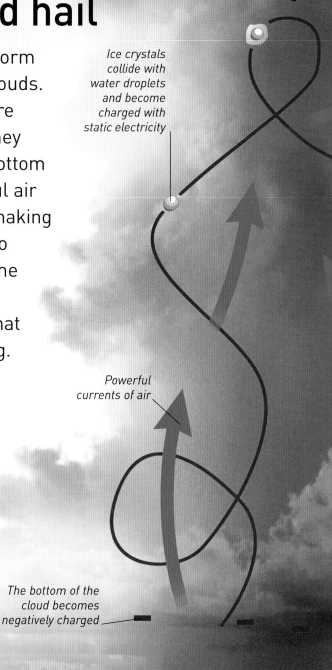

Ice crystals collide with water droplets and become charged with static electricity

Powerful currents of air

The bottom of the cloud becomes negatively charged

Charged up
Strong air currents surging through deep storm clouds charge them up with static electricity. The charge is positive at the top and negative at the bottom, just like a giant battery.

Giant hail
Some parts of the world, such as the American Midwest, suffer from huge hailstones that can be as big as tennis balls. They form inside gigantic storm clouds of the type that often turn into tornadoes. The hailstones fall out of the sky like rocks, and can cause a lot of damage.

Crop damage ▲
A big hailstorm can flatten valuable crops, so there is nothing left to harvest.

Treacherous roads ▲
Hailstones on the road roll beneath cars like ball bearings, and can cause crashes.

The top of the cloud becomes positively charged

Ice crystals are swept around the cloud and get coated with more and more layers of ice

Eventually, the ice crystals become so heavy that they fall from the cloud as hailstones

HAIR RAISING

You can generate your own static electricity by rubbing an inflated balloon against your clothes for a few minutes. If you rub hard, this will build up an electrical charge in the balloon, just like the charge that builds up in a storm cloud. Stand in front of a mirror and hold the charged balloon above your head. Bring it down slowly, and you will see how the electrical charge attracts your hair, making it stand on end. Luckily, the charge is not powerful enough to produce lightning!

Electrostatic attraction ▲
The static electricity creates a force that attracts your hair. It can also attract the balloon to other objects. Try charging the balloon, then throwing it up against the ceiling. What happens to it?

Shattered glass ▲
Giant hailstones are heavy enough to smash glass and dent steel.

◄ Deadly hailstones
Most hailstones are the size of peas or marbles, but the ones shown here are nearly as big as the golf ball next to them. The largest authenticated hailstone in the world fell in Kansas, USA, in 1970 and weighed 0.77 kg (1 lb 11 oz).

Thunderstorms

The charges that build up in storm clouds can reach 100 million volts or more, making huge sparks leap between the cloud and the ground. These begin as faint, forked, and stepped leaders that zig-zag downward. When one leader approaches the ground, a spark leaps up to meet it, and a massive bolt of electricity lights up the leader as a lightning flash. You can simulate the effect by charging up a metal plate and using it to create a spark.

LIGHTNING AND THUNDER

Lightning heats the air within the flash by up to 30,000°C (54,000°F) in less than a second. That's four to five times the surface temperature of the Sun! The intense heat makes the air expand explosively, causing a shockwave that makes the noise we call thunder. There are usually several lightning strokes within a few fractions of a second, and this is why thunder sounds crackly.

Struck by lightning ▲
Lightning usually strikes tall objects such as trees. The intense heat burns a track down the tree and can completely destroy it. Metal lightning conductors stop this happening to buildings.

Forked lightning
The main lightning stroke flashes along one of the fainter leader strokes that fork down from the thunder cloud.

WHAT YOU WILL NEED

- One rubber glove
- Cloth, preferably one made from artificial fibre
- Metal plate or tray
- Kitchen scissors with plastic handles
- Stopwatch

1 **Lay the cloth** on a table. Put the rubber glove on your hand to insulate it, and rub the metal plate lightly against the cloth for several minutes. This should build up a charge of static electricity.

2 **Darken the room.** Very slowly, lower the tips of the scissors towards the metal plate. If the plate is charged up enough, a spark will jump between the plate and the scissor tips, and you may hear a faint crackle of thunder.

HOW NEAR IS THE STORM?

The speed of light is so fast that you see lightning the instant it happens. The speed of sound is slower, so you hear the thunder after the flash. Since sound travels 1 km in 3 seconds (1 mile in 5 seconds), the time difference between the flash and the thunder tells you how near the storm is.

Use a stopwatch ▲
Time the difference with a stopwatch, and then divide the seconds by three (kilometres) or five (miles) to give the distance between you and the storm.

HANDY TIP

Some types of carpet generate static electricity, so you could try rubbing the plate on the floor.

Twisting tornadoes

Big storm clouds contain powerful rising air currents. If these start turning they can create a spiral of rising air, called a vortex. Sometimes the rising vortex becomes so violent that it acts rather like a vacuum cleaner, sucking in the surrounding air at high speed to form a spinning tornado. These twisters affect very small areas compared to hurricanes, but they contain the fastest, most destructive winds on Earth. You can recreate the effect in a glass of spinning fizzy water.

WHAT YOU WILL NEED

- Tall glass tumbler
- Fizzy water, soda, or lemonade
- Free-flowing table salt
- Swizzle stick or long-handled stirrer

Twister
Tornadoes are caused by warm air rising and forming massive storm clouds called supercells. The rising air sucks in more air at ground level, and as the air swirls inward it speeds up to form a tornado.

Rising air spirals upward to form a low-pressure vortex

TORNADO ALLEY

In the USA, the prairie states of Texas, Oklahoma, Kansas, and Nebraska suffer so many destructive tornadoes that they are known as Tornado Alley. In these areas, warm, moist air moving north from the Gulf of Mexico meets cool, dry air moving south from Canada. The two air masses swirl together to create low-pressure cyclones that can generate tornadoes.

Canada

USA

☐ Tornado Alley
☐ Tornadoes also common in these areas

TORNADO DAMAGE

The incredibly low air pressure inside a tornado can create updrafts of up to 240 km/h (150 mph). These rip the roofs off houses, and suck cars into the air and flip them over like toys. The winds swirling into the vortex are also extreme.

Oklahoma City tornado ▶
Windspeeds of 512 km/h (318 mph) were recorded during the 1999 Oklahoma City tornado, which wrecked about 1,500 homes.

1 **Pour the fizzy water**, soda, or lemonade into the glass until it is two-thirds full. Don't put too much in the glass or it will overflow when you stir it.

2 **Use the swizzle stick** to stir the fizzy liquid. Get it spinning fast, then pour some salt into it. The salt makes carbon dioxide bubbles form in the liquid.

3 **Watch the rising** bubbles form a tornado. You can keep repeating this experiment as long as the bubbles keep appearing.

The bubbles swirl round in a spinning vortex

Hurricanes

The most destructive weather events are hurricanes, also known as typhoons or tropical cyclones. These are deep depressions formed by moist air rising off warm oceans, with huge storm clouds and high winds swirling around cores of very low air pressure. The high winds can be extremely destructive, but the worst effects are caused by storm surges of ocean water that sweep over low-lying coasts and islands. See how a storm surge works by creating your own low-pressure system in a bowl of water.

WHAT YOU WILL NEED

- Clear plastic cup
- Scissors or sharp-pointed tool
- Drinking straw
- Sticky putty
- Large washing-up bowl
- Chopping board that fits in the bowl
- Water

Ask an adult to make the hole in the cup.

1 **Use the sharp tool** to make a small hole in the base of the plastic cup, just big enough to take the drinking straw. Be careful not to split the cup.

2 **Push the straw** into the hole from the outside, so a short length is inside the cup. Seal the join with the putty.

TROPICAL REVOLVING STORMS

Hurricane winds swirl around the eye (centre) of the storm at speeds of 120 km/h (75 mph) or more, creating spirals of cloud that are visible from space. Hurricanes form over tropical oceans with surface temperatures of more than 26°C (79°F), and the warmer the water, the more powerful they get.

Hurricane Katrina ▲
You can see the eye of the storm at the centre of this satellite image of Hurricane Katrina, pictured as it came ashore over New Orleans in the USA in 2005. The hurricane destroyed most of the city.

3 **Place the chopping board** inside the bowl. Lean it against one side to make a shallow, sloping "beach" or coastline.

STORM SURGE

The eye of a hurricane has only light winds, but the air pressure within the eye is so low that it sucks in ocean water. This can grow into a wall of water up to 10 m (33 ft) high as it approaches the land, smashing into the coast like a tsunami.

Flood victims ▶
Survivors of Hurricane Katrina seek safety on top of a car. New Orleans was mostly built below sea level, making it prone to flooding.

4 **Fill the bowl** with water and place the cup upside-down on the board, with the rim slightly under the surface. Notice that the water level is the same inside and out. Suck on the straw to reduce the air pressure inside the cup. This creates the same kind of low-pressure zone that occurs in the core of a hurricane.

Sucking on the straw creates low pressure

Low pressure raises the water level

5 **Put your fingertip** over the straw, and move the cup up the "beach". You can see that the water level is much higher than the "coast", and when the cup reaches the "shore", the water can spill out to cause a flood.

The seasons

Most parts of the world have different seasons, such as winter and summer. This is because the Earth spins on a tilted axis. As the tilted Earth orbits the Sun, the northern and southern regions move towards the Sun or away from it. This makes them warmer and brighter in summer, and cooler and darker in the winter. You can make a model of the orbiting Earth using an orange and an ordinary table lamp.

WHAT YOU WILL NEED

- 1 small orange
- Kitchen skewer
- Table lamp with shade removed
- Marker pen

Ask an adult to help with the skewer and when removing the lamp shade.

1 **Push the** kitchen skewer through the core of the orange, and mark two crosses as shown.

North pole

2 **Switch on** the table lamp and darken the rest of the room. The lamp represents the Sun. Hold the orange on one side of the "Sun" with its axis at a slight angle (see left), to represent the tilted Earth in June.

3 **Spin the "Earth"** slowly on its axis. The cross at the equator moves in and out of the light as night follows day. The cross near the top does the same, but spends longer in the daylight. It is also facing the Sun directly at midday.

Equator

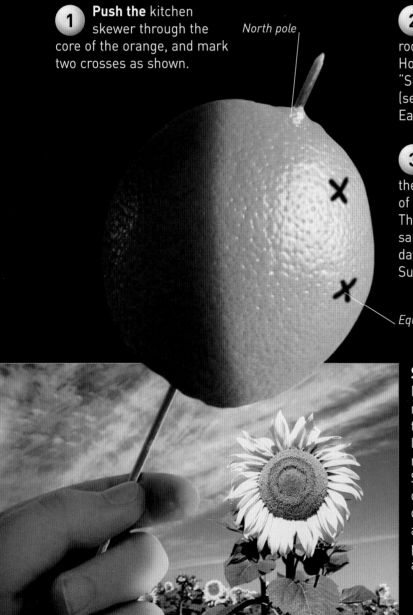

Summer sunshine
Near the equator, the days are always roughly the same length. But nearer the North or South Pole, days get longer in summer. These temperate regions are also tilted towards the Sun in summer, so the Sun is high overhead and heats the ground more directly. So summer days are longer and warmer than winter days. In the polar regions it doesn't get dark at all at midsummer.

TROPICAL MONSOONS

The tropical regions also have seasons. In the southern summer the Sun shines over the Indian Ocean, warming the air and making it rise and form huge rain clouds. The rising air draws cool, dry air south over India from central Asia. Six months later the intense sunshine and rising air has moved north of India. It draws warm, wet air off the ocean, causing monsoon rains.

Torrential rain ▶
The monsoon rain that falls on India is so heavy that it often causes serious flooding. Yet it also provides vital water for growing crops. If the monsoon comes late, many crops may fail.

4 **Move the Earth** to the other side of the Sun, but keep its axis tilted the same way. Spin the Earth. The cross near the equator is not affected by the change, but the cross further north spends less time in the daylight and never faces the Sun directly. This is what happens in December, in the northern winter.

In December, northern regions have short winter days

In December, southern regions have long summer days

Winter snow
When temperate regions are tilted away from the Sun, the days are shorter and the nights are longer. The Sun's energy is also spread out over a wider area, so it doesn't heat the ground so much. This gives the shorter, cooler days of winter. The temperature can fall way below freezing, especially in the far north and the far south. In the polar regions there is permanent darkness in the middle of winter.

Ice mirrors

Snow and ice act like mirrors, reflecting the light and heat of the Sun rather than absorbing its energy and melting. This is called the "albedo effect". If a cold region develops an ice sheet, its albedo increases, so it absorbs less heat and gets colder. The result can be an ice age. You can use black and white card to show how this works.

1 **Fill both** plastic trays with dry sand until they are overflowing. Then scrape the ruler across the top of the sand to level it. The sand should fill each tray to the rim.

2 **Place the sheet** of black paper on one tray of levelled sand, and the sheet of white paper on the other tray. Make sure they are touching the sand. You may need to weigh the paper down if it is a breezy day.

FREEZE-UP AND MELTDOWN

If a cooling climate makes an ice sheet grow, it reflects more solar energy and makes the world even colder. But if climate change makes part of an ice sheet melt, the exposed dark rock absorbs more solar energy and warms up. This makes more ice melt, exposing more dark rock, which absorbs more heat. Eventually, this could cause runaway meltdown, so the ice sheet disappears altogether.

◄ **Spring thaw**
Melting snow in early spring reveals tough mountain plants growing high in the Chilean Andes, South America. As the dark plants and rocks absorb energy, they heat up and warm the air. This speeds up the thaw, until by summer only the highest peaks are still capped with snow.

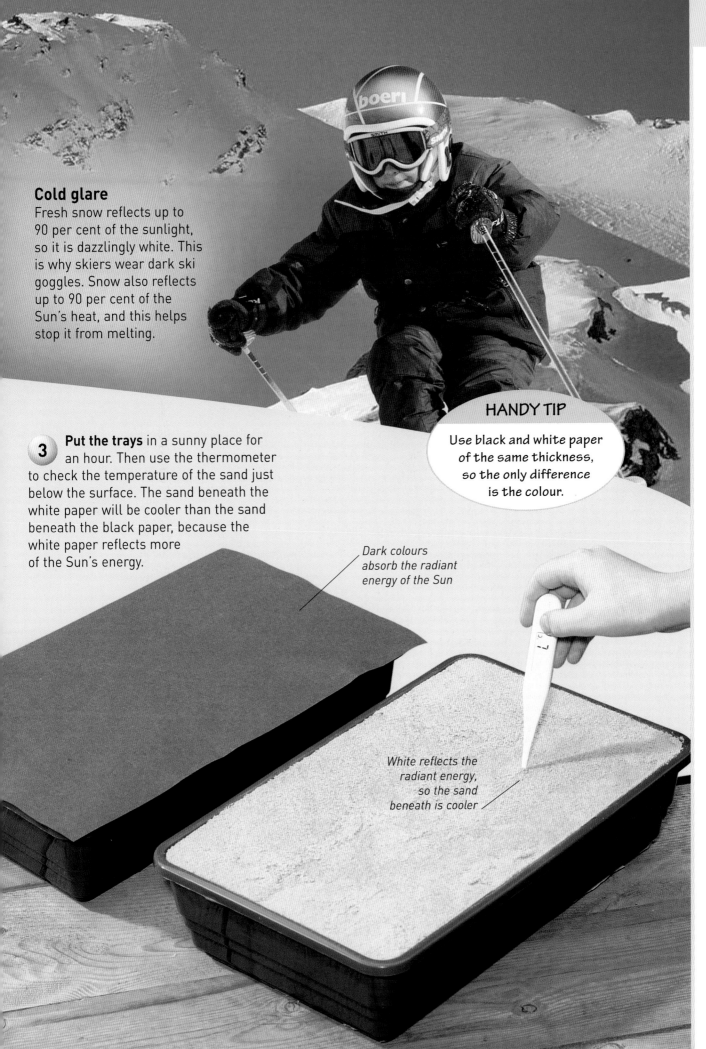

Cold glare

Fresh snow reflects up to 90 per cent of the sunlight, so it is dazzlingly white. This is why skiers wear dark ski goggles. Snow also reflects up to 90 per cent of the Sun's heat, and this helps stop it from melting.

3 **Put the trays** in a sunny place for an hour. Then use the thermometer to check the temperature of the sand just below the surface. The sand beneath the white paper will be cooler than the sand beneath the black paper, because the white paper reflects more of the Sun's energy.

HANDY TIP

Use black and white paper of the same thickness, so the only difference is the colour.

Dark colours absorb the radiant energy of the Sun

White reflects the radiant energy, so the sand beneath is cooler

Plants and rain

Plants soak up water and use it to make sugar. Some of the water evaporates into the air through their leaves, and this draws more water into their roots, along with dissolved plant foods. Trees pump vast amounts of water back into the air like this. It is an invisible process, but you can make it visible by covering a plant with a plastic bag.

WHAT YOU WILL NEED

- Leafy pot plant
- Large, clear plastic bag
- String
- Saucer of water

1 **Turn the bag** upside down and carefully lower it over the plant. Enclose all the leaves, then use the string to tie the bag around the stems, leaving the soil exposed to the air.

2 **Put the plant back** in the place where it was growing well. Put the saucer of water under the pot and leave the plant for a few days. Keep the soil moist.

AIR CONDITIONING

In tropical rainforests the trees help to form the clouds and rain that keep them alive. They almost create their own climate. If large areas of rainforest are cut down, the climate in the region often becomes drier, because the trees are no longer pumping moisture back into the air.

Steamy rainforest ▶
The air in rainforests is very humid, partly because of all the moisture evaporating from the trees.

Leaves and climate

If plants lose too much water to the air, they wilt and die. Plants that live in hot, dry climates have developed methods of reducing the amount of water they lose. In wet climates, it is less essential for plants to conserve water, and plants tend to have leaves with a bigger surface area.

Big leaves ▶

Most plants with big, broad leaves lose a lot of water, so they are suited to wet climates. Such leaves are easily destroyed by frost, so in regions with cold winters, many plants drop their leaves in autumn and grow a new set in spring.

◀ Small leaves

In places with dry summers or long winters, many trees have small, waxy, needle-shaped leaves. These lose moisture less easily than big leaves, and can survive frosty weather.

3 **The bag will** steam up with moisture on the inside. Since the bag does not cover the moist soil, all this moisture must be evaporating from the leaves of the plant itself.

No leaves ▶

Many plants that naturally grow in deserts have no obvious leaves. A cactus, for example, soaks up water like a sponge whenever it gets the chance, and loses as little moisture as possible to the dry desert air.

HANDY TIP

Don't put the plant in strong sunlight. It will get too hot inside the bag.

The "leaves" of a cactus have become sharp spines

Why is the sky blue?

Air is a mixture of colourless, transparent gases, so why is the sky blue, and why does it turn red at sunset? The reason is to do with the fact that white sunlight is a mixture of all the colours of the rainbow. Gas molecules and dust in the atmosphere scatter the white light, splitting it into the rainbow colours. Blue light is scattered most strongly, so the sky appears to be blue. You can create the same effect by shining white light through milky water.

WHAT YOU WILL NEED

- Large, clear glass bottle or jar with lid
- Water
- Milk
- Teaspoon
- Torch
- 2–3 thick books

1 **Pour water** into the bottle or jar until it is nearly full and add about half a teaspoon of milk. Put the lid on the jar and shake until the milk and water are mixed together.

You need only a small amount of milk to begin with

BLUE SKY

A blue sky is caused by air molecules scattering sunlight. This scattering is greatest at the violet and blue end of the spectrum of colours that make up white light. Since our eyes are not very sensitive to violet, we see only the blue that has been split off from the white light. The same effect is created by milk particles in the experiment.

Deep blue sky ▲
A lot of water vapour in the air makes the sky look paler blue, so the deepest blue colour is usually seen when recent rain or frost have swept most of the water vapour out of the sky.

RED SUNSET

When the Sun is close to the horizon at sunset, you are seeing it through a lot more of the atmosphere than when it is overhead. This means that its light passes through more air. The air scatters the blue light so much that it cannot be seen at all. As a result, the Sun and sky look red.

◄ Fiery glow
All the air between you and the setting Sun bends the light as well as altering its colour. It makes the Sun seem bigger, and distorts it into a wavy oval shape. It also cuts down the glare, so you can look straight at it.

2 **Prop up the torch** on the books so it is shining through the jar from the side. Look at the water from the front. Turn the torch off or away, and then back on again. Does the milky water seem a different colour? If not, add more milk until the mixture starts to look pale blue, like sky.

3 **Once you can see** the blue light, try adding more milk to the mixture. The colour will change from blue to faint orange, rather like the sky at sunset.

HANDY TIP
If you can't see the red sunset effect, try looking directly at the light beam through the container.

Acid rain

Rain is naturally slightly acidic. This is because water vapour dissolves carbon dioxide in the air to form weak carbonic acid. But rain can become more acidic if the air is polluted with oxides of nitrogen and sulphur. These mix with water vapour to form weak nitric and sulphuric acid. If this falls as rain, it can poison lakes and kill trees. Acid rain also gradually destroys objects made of limestone, because the acid dissolves the stone. You can see this happening using vinegar and chalk.

1 **Place the lump** of chalk or concrete on the metal tray. Chalk has the same composition as natural limestone. Concrete contains limestone that has been turned into cement.

2 **Pour some** of the vinegar onto your lump of rock. You won't need to use much. This imitates acid rain falling on limestone.

DEADLY ACID

The worst effects of acid rain are felt in the far north, in places such as Canada, Norway, and Sweden. The acid is carried on the wind from nearby industrial countries, and falls on areas where the rocks are very hard and do not contain any lime. Reacting with lime would make the acid harmless, but because this does not happen, the acid rain is washed into rivers and lakes, killing all the fish.

Poisoned trees ▲
Large areas of forest are dying in many parts of northern Europe. This may be a result of acid rain damage, or it may be caused by air and rain being poisoned by some other type of pollution.

WHAT YOU WILL NEED

- Lump of chalk or concrete
- Vinegar
- Metal baking tray
- Magnifying glass

Eroded carvings
Many old churches are built from limestone, and they are often decorated with sculptures. Where acid rain is a problem, the acid dissolves the carvings so they look like shapeless lumps of rock.

The detail of this carved face has been eroded by acid rain

3 **The rock will** start to fizz as the acid starts to dissolve it. The process releases bubbles of carbon dioxide, just like those in a fizzy drink. You can hear the fizz, but unless your vinegar is very acidic you will need the magnifying glass to see the bubbles.

Carbon dioxide bubbles from the rock

HANDY TIP
You can use this activity as a test to find out if a piece of rock is a type of limestone.

The greenhouse effect

The atmosphere forms an invisible blanket around the Earth. It allows the Sun's energy to pass through and warm the land and sea, but stops heat from escaping back into space. Carbon dioxide, water vapour, and some other gases in the air absorb the heat instead. This keeps us warm, and without it the Earth would be too cold for life to exist. As the gases absorb heat, they warm up, setting the weather systems of the world in motion. This is called the greenhouse effect, because the gases trap heat like the glass of a greenhouse. You can create your own greenhouse effect in a bottle.

WHAT YOU WILL NEED

- Big soda bottle
- Jam jar
- Scissors
- Thermometer
  Ask an adult to cut the bottle.

1 **Use the scissors** to cut the bottom off the plastic bottle. Strip off the paper label, but leave the top screwed on. This is your greenhouse.

2 **Stand the** thermometer inside the jar. Then place it in a sunny spot, and check the temperature after an hour.

GLOBAL WARMING

Burning coal, oil, gas, and other fossil fuels is adding carbon dioxide to the atmosphere. This increases the greenhouse effect, and makes the world warmer. The extra warmth is likely to make the weather more extreme, and could dramatically change the climate in many parts of the world.

Fossil fuels ▲
Fossil fuels contain carbon that was absorbed from the air more than 200 million years ago, before dinosaurs existed. Burning carbon turns it into carbon dioxide.

3 **Put the** bottle greenhouse over the jar, and leave it for another hour. When you check the temperature you will find it is higher, because solar energy passing into the bottle has been turned into heat that cannot escape. Greenhouse gases in the atmosphere trap heat in a similar way.

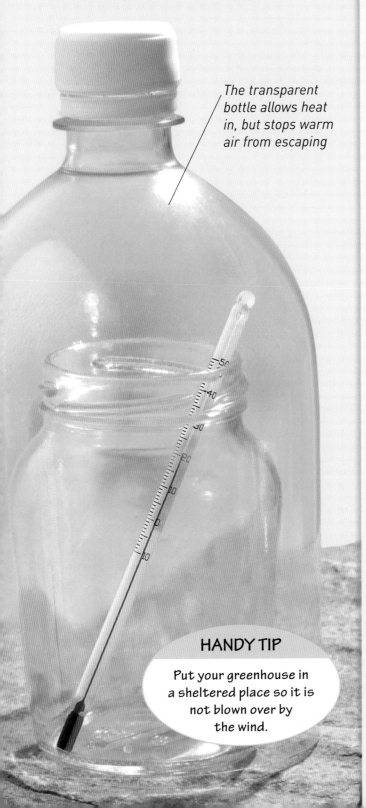

The transparent bottle allows heat in, but stops warm air from escaping

HANDY TIP

Put your greenhouse in a sheltered place so it is not blown over by the wind.

Climate change

Global warming sounds like it might improve the weather, but it will actually make it worse. The warmer the atmosphere, the more violent the weather. Expanding oceans will also cause flooding.

Hurricane winds ▲
As ocean temperatures rise, the hurricane zone will spread further north and south, and hurricanes will get more severe. There will be frequent and heavier rainstorms as more water evaporates from the warm oceans.

Drought ▲
As continents warm up, moisture will evaporate from the ground more quickly. It will form big storm clouds in some places. Other areas will suffer deadly droughts that will ruin crops and cause famines.

Ice and snow ▲
Heavier rain and melting ice may change the way some ocean currents flow. This could make some regions, such as northern Europe, colder than they have been since the last ice age ended more than 10,000 years ago.

Weather forecasting

Weather forecasters collect information gathered by weather stations over a wide area, and plot it on maps. The atmospheric pressure readings are particularly useful, because they mark weather systems such as cyclones, which bring wind and rain. Every few hours new data is plotted on a new map. This shows how the weather systems are moving, where they might be going, and what the weather may be like.

Occluded front
A cold front has caught up with a warm front, lifting warm air off the ground. This can produce heavy rain.

Weather map
Places where the atmospheric pressure is the same are joined by lines called isobars. The isobars form rings around centres of low pressure and high pressure. The low-pressure centres contain warm and cold fronts. These are also marked on the map, and indicate places where there is likely to be a lot of cloud and rain.

1008
LOW
1016
1024
1024
1016
1008
1000
1032
992
LOW
HIGH

KEEP TRACK OF THE WEATHER

Cut out the weather maps from a daily newspaper for a week, and see how the changing weather pattern fits in with the actual weather you get. Watch how the low-pressure zones and weather fronts move over your area, and see what effect they have. After five days, see if you can work out what the weather may do next.

Monday   Tuesday   Wednesday Thursday   Friday   Saturday   Sunday

A week of weather ▲
Keep a note of the weather forecast and the actual weather. How accurate is the forecast? Is it mostly right or wrong?

Cold front
A cold front is marked with blue triangles. The weather is cloudy ahead of the front, but clears when the front passes.

Low-pressure zone
Rings of isobars with the lowest pressure near the centre mark a low-pressure zone, cyclone, or depression. The weather is usually dull and rainy, with strong winds.

HIGH

1032

024

1024

1016

1008

2

1040

HIGH

WEATHER STATION

Most of the data used by forecasters is gathered by automatic weather stations and satellites. Yet weather data can also be collected using quite simple instruments, such as the barometer, anemometer, wind vane, and rain gauge featured in this book. Accurate versions of these instruments are used throughout the world. The data is recorded by hand, but it can be just as useful as the information collected automatically.

Stevenson screen ▲
Some of the instruments used for gathering weather data are kept in a white, ventilated box called a Stevenson screen. This protects the instruments from the effects of wind and direct sunshine.

Isobars
These link places where the atmospheric pressure is the same. On this map every other isobar is marked with the pressure in millibars.

Warm front
A warm front is marked with red semicircles. As a warm front approaches, the weather gets cloudy and rainy, and stays dull as the front passes.

High-pressure zone
Rings of isobars with the highest pressure near the centre mark a high-pressure zone or anticyclone, where it is usually cloudless and sunny.

Weather technology

Today a lot of weather data is collected by high-technology devices. These include satellites equipped with specialized scanners. The information is beamed back from space, fed into computers, and turned into images of weather systems. Computers are also used to produce weather forecasts from all the data gathered by satellites and automatic weather stations. These computer-generated images and forecasts are available on the Internet, and it is easy to access them using your own computer.

Data processing
Powerful computers speed up the processing of weather data. A lot of data is used, making weather forecasts very accurate.

HANDY TIP

Try using words such as "hail" and "tornado" in your search. You might find something exciting!

1. **Use a search engine** to locate a website devoted to weather and climate. You can often type in your address, or part of it, to focus on the weather in your area.

2. **Check the forecast** for the week ahead. Look at any weather maps or satellite images that are available. Some websites show animations of satellite images. Can you see how they relate to the forecast?

3. **Look for any** information about the weather pattern. There are often special web pages about the weather systems affecting your area. Check out any features on weather events worldwide, such as hurricanes or droughts.

The balloon expands as it rises higher into the air

STORM CHASERS

Some people enjoy watching and filming extreme weather. They are called storm chasers. Many storm chasers follow the thunderstorms and tornadoes that hit the American Midwest. You can join in by checking their websites on the Internet.

Chasing a storm ▲
Many storm chasers use laptop computers to keep track of the weather. They can work out where the next big storm is likely to happen, get out there, and wait for it to build up.

WEATHER SATELLITES

There are two types of weather satellite. Some orbit the Earth at a very high level, and complete one orbit every 24 hours. This means they stay over one place all the time. Others orbit at lower levels, and cover the whole planet every five days.

Taking off ▲
Weather satellites are launched into space using powerful rockets. They are controlled from Earth, but carry out many tasks automatically.

◄ Weather balloon
Weather researchers use balloons to carry weather instruments high into the sky. This balloon will rise to a height of about 24 km (15 miles) and radio back data on temperature, humidity, and atmospheric pressure.

Antarctic weather station ▲
There are weather researchers working all over the world, in weather stations such as this one in Antarctica. Many other weather stations are completely automatic.

Glossary

Air pressure The squeezing effect of the weight of air in the atmosphere (also known as atmospheric pressure). Rising warm air weighs less, so gives low air pressure. Sinking cool air gives high air pressure.

Albedo A measure of the way surfaces, such as clouds and rock, reflect the Sun's energy. Very reflective surfaces have high albedo. Less reflective surfaces have low albedo.

Altostratus Mid-level, sheet-like clouds.

Anemometer An instrument for measuring wind speed.

Anticyclone A weather system with high air pressure at its centre, usually with clear, cloudless skies.

Atmosphere The blanket of mixed gases that surrounds the Earth. It has several layers.

Barometer An instrument for measuring air pressure.

Carbon dioxide A gas used by plants to make sugar, and produced by animals in the reaction that turns sugar into energy. It exists in very small quantities in the atmosphere.

Cirrus High, wispy cloud.

Climate The average weather in a particular place.

Cold front The boundary between cold and warm air masses, created when the cold air pushes under the warm air.

Condensation The process of gas turning into liquid. When water vapour turns into liquid water, it condenses.

Condensation nuclei Tiny particles in the atmosphere that attract water vapour and make it turn into droplets of liquid water.

Contract To get smaller.

Convection Movement in a gas or liquid, caused by heat making some of it warmer, less dense, and lighter, so it rises through the rest.

Coriolis effect The effect of the spinning Earth on the way air masses and weather systems, for example, move across Earth's surface.

Cumulonimbus Very deep storm clouds that rise from low level to high level, and produce heavy rain, lightning, and hail.

Cumulus Heaped, often fluffy-looking, low-level clouds.

Cyclone A weather system with low air pressure at its centre, and warm and cold fronts that create wind, clouds, and rain.

Depression *See* **Cyclone**.

Dew Drops of water produced by water vapour condensing onto cold surfaces overnight.

Equator The imaginary line around the centre of the Earth that marks its widest point. Equatorial regions are very hot.

Evaporation The process of liquid turning into gas, or vapour. When water turns into water vapour, it evaporates.

Expand To get bigger.

Fossil fuels The remains of ancient plants and animals that have been turned into energy-rich coal, oil, and gas.

Glaze Glassy ice.

Greenhouse effect The process by which heat, radiated from the ground, is trapped by gases in the atmosphere, such as carbon dioxide, leading to global warming.

Humidity A measure of the amount of water vapour in the air. Warm air can hold more water vapour, so is often more humid than cold air.

Hurricane A tropical revolving storm with very low air pressure and very strong winds. Also known as a tropical cyclone or typhoon.

Hygrometer An instrument for measuring humidity.

Infrared radiation An invisible form of energy that has a longer wavelength than visible light. We feel it as heat.

Isobar A line on a weather map that joins places with the same air pressure.

Mesosphere A layer of the upper atmosphere, lying between the stratosphere and the thermosphere.

Millibar A unit used as a measure of air pressure.

Molecule A particle formed from atoms. Two hydrogen atoms joined to one oxygen atom form a water molecule.

Monsoon A seasonal wind pattern that brings heavy rain for part of the year, especially in southern Asia.

Nimbostratus A sheet-like rain cloud.

Nimbus A rain cloud.

Nitrogen The gas that forms 78 per cent of the atmosphere.

Occlusion When a mass of warm air is pushed off the ground by a cold front catching up with a warm front.

Oceanic Land regions that are close to oceans, and often have mild, damp climates.

Oxide A substance that is partly made of oxygen. Carbon dioxide is a gas made of carbon and oxygen.

Oxygen The gas that forms 21 per cent of the air. It is released by plants, and used by animals to turn food into energy.

Ozone A form of oxygen gas that exists in a layer in the stratosphere. This layer absorbs harmful ultraviolet radiation.

Polar front The northern and southern polar fronts are the boundaries between cold polar air and warm tropical air.

Polar regions The regions around the North Pole and South Pole, where freezing winters and cold summers create permanent ice.

Rime Thick deposits of ice crystals caused by freezing fog.

Solar radiation The energy of the Sun, which is mainly visible light and invisible infrared and ultraviolet rays.

Spectrum The rainbow pattern produced by splitting white light into separate colours.

Static electricity The electric charge that builds up as a result of friction in storm clouds, and causes lightning.

Storm surge A rise in sea level at the centre of a storm, caused by reduced air pressure.

Stratosphere The layer of the atmosphere that lies above the lowest layer.

Stratus Sheets of cloud.

Sublimation The process in which a solid turns directly to a gas without passing through a liquid phase, or the other way around. For example, ice turning to water vapour.

Subtropics The warm regions of the world to the north and south of the tropics.

Temperate Neither too hot nor too cold. Used to describe the regions to the north and south of the warm subtropics.

Thermal A warm, rising air current.

Thermosphere The outer layer of the atmosphere.

Tornado A violent revolving storm with extremely low air pressure and very strong winds that covers a small area.

Trade winds Steady winds that blow towards the west over tropical oceans. They were important to trading ships in the days of sail.

Tropics The hot regions of the world that lie between the Tropic of Cancer and the Tropic of Capricorn.

Troposphere The lowest layer of the atmosphere, where all the weather happens.

Tundra The treeless lands surrounding the polar ice sheets, which are frozen in winter but thaw in summer.

Ultraviolet radiation An invisible form of energy that has a shorter wavelength than visible light.

Vortex A swirling funnel of water or air, as seen when water swirls down a plughole.

Warm front The boundary between warm and cold air masses, created when the warm air slides up over the cold air.

Water vapour The invisible gas that is formed when liquid water evaporates.

Index

Model Jack Williams
Index Hilary Bird

The publisher would like to thank the following for their kind permission to reproduce their photographs:

(Key: a-above; b-below/bottom; c-centre; f-far; l-left; r-right; t-top)
4 **FLPA - Images of Nature:** Michael & Patricia Fogden/Minden Pictures (cb). **Science Photo Library:** P.G. Adam, Publiphoto Diffusion (br). **4-5 Getty Images:** Photographer's Choice. **5 Corbis:** Anthony Redpath (bl); Kit Kittle (cb). **Getty Images:** AFP (tr). **FLPA - Images of Nature:** Christiana Carvalho (br). **6 Science Photo Library:** NASA (bl). **7 Alamy Images:** Royal Geographical Society (cr). **14 Corbis:** Duomo (bl). **15 Corbis:** Philip James Corwin (tr). **20** Avpix/Hugh W. Cowin: (bl) background. **Corbis:** Matthias Kulka (bl). **21 Science Photo Library:** NRSC LTD (tl). **22 Science Photo Library:** Paul Rapson (tr). **24 Science Photo Library:** Damien Lovegrove (cr). **25 Corbis:** Scott T. Smith (tl). **26 FLPA - Images of Nature:** Martin B Withers (br). **27 Getty Images:** Science Faction (cr). **FLPA - Images of Nature:** Mark Moffett/Minden Pictures (bl); Tui De Roy/Minden

Pictures (br). **30 Corbis:** Onne van der Wal (bl). **30-31 Corbis:** Onne van der Wal. **32 Alamy Images:** Photofusion Picture Library (bl). **32-33 Corbis:** Kevin Schafer. **33 Science Photo Library:** Colin Cuthbert (cra); David R. Frazier (br); Pascal Goetghluck (crb); Pekka Parviainen (cl). **36 Science Photo Library:** University of Dundee (cb). **36-37 Corbis:** Roger Tidman. **37 Alamy Images:** Phototake Inc. (cl). **38 Getty Images:** Alan R Moller (c), (tl). **39 Alamy Images:** David R. Frazier Photolibrary, Inc (cr); Troy and Mary Parlee (c). **Corbis:** (cl). **42 Science Photo Library:** Lester V. Bergman (cl). **43 Science Photo Library:** David Parker (br). **44 Alamy Images:** K-Photos. **Corbis:** Lester V. Bergman (cl). **45 Alamy Images:** Alaska Stock LLC (tl). **46 Corbis:** David Gray/Reuters (br). **FLPA - Images of Nature:** J C Allen and Son (cb). **Science Photo Library:** Jim Reed (br). **46-47 Corbis** Michael S. Yamashita. **47 Corbis:** Eric Nguyen/Jim Reed Photography (bc); Roy McMahon (cr). **50-51 Corbis:** Reuters. **51 Science Photo Library:** Jim Reed (tr). **52 Alamy Images:** ImageState. **Science Photo Library:** NOAA (bl). **53 Empics Ltd:** (tr). **54 Corbis:** David Higgs (bl). **55 Corbis:** Ray Juno (br). **Science Photo Library:** Paolo Koch (tr). **56 Alamy Images:** Des

Kilfeather (bl). **56-57 Alamy Images:** Buzz Pictures. **57 Corbis:** Duomo (tr). **58 Corbis:** Paul A. Souders (bc). **59 Corbis:** Craig Tuttle (cra); Douglas Faulkner (cr). **60 Corbis:** William Manning (bl). **61 Corbis:** Lester Lefkowitz (tl). **62 Corbis:** Will & Deni McIntyre (bl). **63 Corbis:** Jim Winkley/Ecoscene (tr). **64 Alamy Images:** allOver photography (bl). **65 Corbis:** Jim Reed (tr). **Science Photo Library:** Jerry Irwin (cr); Simon Fraser (br). **66 Getty Images:** Alan Kearney (tl). **67 Science Photo Library:** David hay Jones (cr). **68 Alamy Images:** Stock Connection Distribution (tr). **68 Corbis:** Michael Prince (b). **69 Corbis:** Danny Gawlowski/Dallas Morning News (cra). **Science Photo Library:** British Antarctic Survey. **74 Dreamstime.com:** Andreiuc88 (cla). **75 Dorling Kindersley:** Emma Firth (tr). Dreamstime.com: Delmas Lehman (ca); Dustine Meads (cra). Fotolia: Zee (cl). **78 Dreamstime.com:** Sergey Kichigin (cl, ca); Joao Virissimo (tl); Miramisska (cb); Vladimir Melnik (crb). PunchStock: Image Source (tr). **79 Dreamstime.com:** Sergey Kichigin (cra); Benjamin Todd Shoemake (cb). Fotolia: Silver (c)

All other images © Dorling Kindersley
For further information see: **www.dkimages.com**